SPARK ISLAND

KS2 National Tests
SCIENCE
Learning Adventures

Contents

Introduction	2
Practice questions	
Green plants	4
Living things and their environments	6
The human body	9
Electricity	12
Forces	14
Light	18
Sound and vibration	20
The Earth and beyond	22
Grouping and classifying materials	24
Changing materials	26
Separating mixtures of materials	28
Practice test	29
Sample test questions and answers	39
Answers to practice questions	43
Answers to practice test	46
Glossary	48

Simon Greaves

Introduction

The National Tests

In May all pupils in Year 6 take National Tests. They are designed to be an objective assessment of the work covered from Year 3 up to Year 6 and the results of these, together with assessment by the teachers, give a clear picture of children's overall achievement.

In Science there are two tests: Test A and Test B. Children are allowed 45 minutes for Test A and 45 minutes for Test B.

What is covered in the tests?

There are four main areas:

- life and living things - all about humans, other animals and plants
- materials and their properties - all about different materials and how they are used in everyday life
- physical processes - all about electricity, forces, light, sound and our planet
- scientific enquiry - all about doing and using data from experiments and investigations.

Topics can appear in any test. Most of the Key Stage 2 material will be tested but it is impossible for the tests to cover everything.

What are the questions like?

You will see from the practice questions section (pages 4-28) that there are several different styles of question. These are some typical styles:

- A question with several 'tick box' answers where children are asked to tick a number of boxes. They need to make sure they only tick the number of boxes asked for. If they tick more they will lose marks.
- A question asking them to join lines between boxes or pictures. They should make sure the lines are clearly drawn but it's a good idea for children to complete the test in pencil so they can rub out any mistakes.
- A diagram which needs completing or where labels need to be filled in.
- A graph or table which needs to be completed, or from which information needs to be read.
- A question asking for an explanation. The answer must include certain important words and shouldn't simply repeat the question in a different way.

Helping your child to prepare for the tests

Think about the best time for working. It might be easier at a weekend or early in the evening. Most of all, pick a time when your child is eager to learn and not too tired. Find a suitable place where he or she can work comfortably without being disturbed, then make a start on the practice questions.

When you think you have revised all the topics, your child can try the practice test in this book (pages 29-38). Mark it using the answers at the back of the book and then look at any wrong answers together. This will highlight any topics that need a bit more work. After some more revision your child can try the test again.

There are detailed answers, at the back of the book, for all the practice questions. Make sure that you go through your child's incorrect answers and explain what he or she did wrong. Help him or her to work out what would have been a good answer.

There are detailed answers too for the practice test (marked out of 40). You can use the scoring table (page 47) to work out an approximate level for your child's performance.

At the back of this book (pages 39-42), there are some sample test questions taken from the 2002 National Science Tests together with sample answers. These give some guidance on what makes a good and bad answer. These can be used to help explain the best way to answer test questions.

What will children feel like on the day of the tests?

If they have done some preparation they should feel confident and may even be looking forward to the challenge of the tests. Try not to make them over-confident so that they rush through the tests without reading the questions properly and make careless mistakes.

Even if they have done lots of work they may still feel nervous. Tell them to remember the work they have put in. It's all up there in their head so remind them to relax, take a few deep breaths and take their time. Once they've started they will probably feel more confident.

How will I find out how my child has done?

The tests are sent away to be marked. The school will get the scores around the start of July. The teacher will then tell your child their level and you will receive a report.

Green plants

Bright sparks!

- A plant needs light, air, water and warmth to grow.
- The roots take up water and **nutrients** and anchor the plant in the ground.
- Green plants make their own food in their leaves.
- Flowers produce **pollen**. Pollen is needed to fertilize a plant's eggs.
- Fertilized eggs become seeds which are dispersed in many ways.

Did you know that seeds can be **dispersed** by wind, animals and by explosion of pods?

seeds stuck to fur
seeds stuck to feet
seeds in droppings

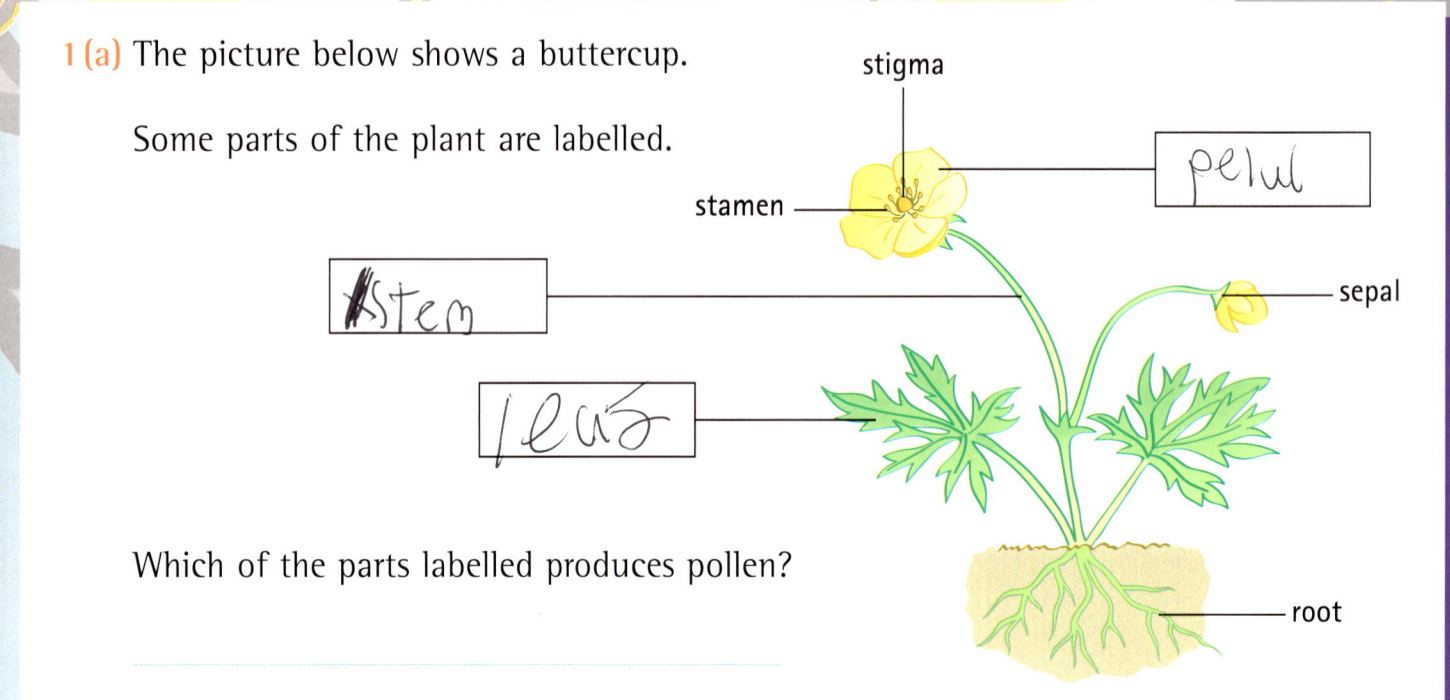

1 (a) The picture below shows a buttercup.

Some parts of the plant are labelled.

stigma — petal
stamen
Stem
leaf
sepal
root

Which of the parts labelled produces pollen?

(b) Complete the missing labels.

(c) Explain how the roots help the plant to grow well.

2 (a) The picture shows a dandelion at the stage in its life cycle when it has produced seeds.

close-up of seed

To continue its life cycle the dandelion must disperse (scatter) its seeds.

What feature of the seeds suggests that they are dispersed by the wind?

_____

_____

(b) Which of the following words describes the dandelion?

Tick **ONE** box.   Prey ☐   Producer ☐   Predator ☐   Consumer ✓

3 (a) Strat planted four dandelion seeds in pots.
The seeds **germinated** and grew into small plants.
Strat grew the plants under different conditions.

Plant A   watered every day, kept in a warm, dark cupboard

Plant B   not watered, kept on a warm, sunny windowsill

Plant C   watered every day, kept on a warm, sunny windowsill

Plant D   watered every hour, kept on a cool, sunny windowsill

Which plant do you think grew better than the others?

Tick **ONE** box.   Plant A ☐   Plant B ✗   Plant C ✓   Plant D ☐

(b) Give a reason for your answer.

because its get water and sun evey day

Living things and their environments

Bright sparks!

- Animals and plants have special features which make them more suitable for living in different **habitats**.

- A food chain shows what eats what. Most food chains begin with a green plant.

- Micro-organisms are living things which are too small to be seen without a microscope. Some are helpful and some are harmful.

What do you mean by habitat?

It's just another word for home.

In a food chain plants are **producers** because they make their own food.

Animals are **consumers** because they eat other plants and animals.

Predators are animals which eat other animals (**prey**).

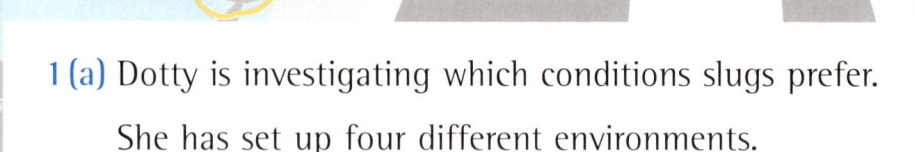

---

1 (a) Dotty is investigating which conditions slugs prefer.

She has set up four different environments.

A — dry sand

B — dry sand, covered with card

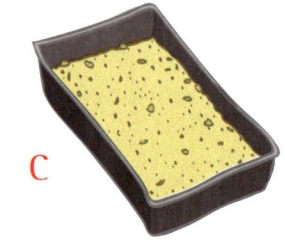

C — damp soil

D — damp soil, covered with card

Which environment will the slugs prefer?

Write A, B, C or D in the box. **C**

(b) Give ONE reason for your answer.

Slugs like wet and soggy sludg

6

(c) Slugs are one of the consumers in a food chain.

Put these living things into the correct order in the food chain.

cabbage   kestrel   slug   thrush

| slug | → | Cabbage | → | Kestrel | → | thrush |

(d) Which of the four living things is the producer in the food chain? ~~thrush~~ ~~thrush~~ cabbage

2 Which three things do all living things do?

Tick **THREE** boxes.

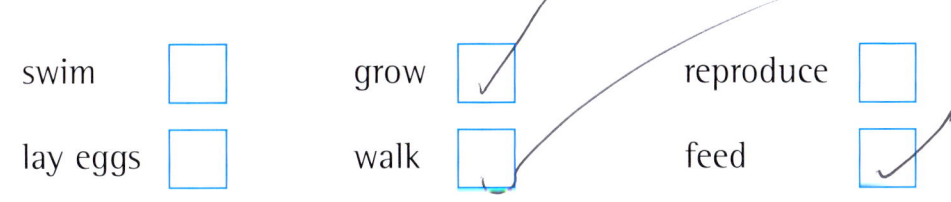

- swim ☐
- grow ☑
- reproduce ☐
- lay eggs ☐
- walk ☐
- feed ☑

(Note: only two boxes ticked, arrow drawn from grow toward reproduce)

3 (a) Look at the five beetles in the picture below.

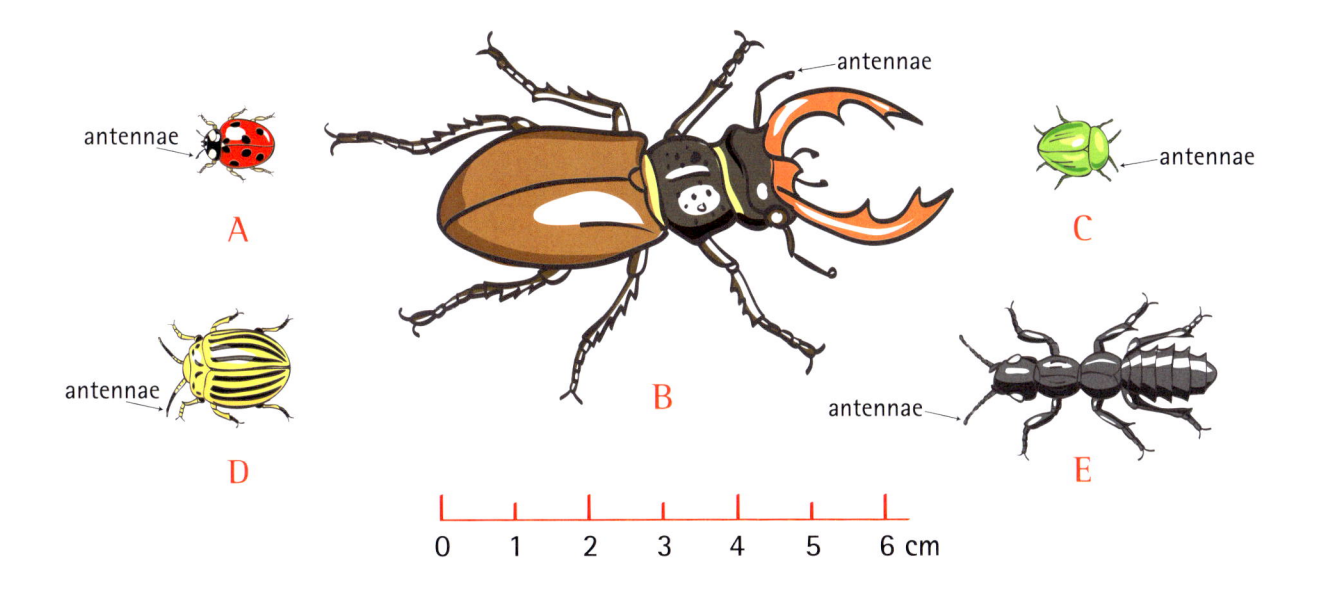

Use the key on the next page to identify beetle C.

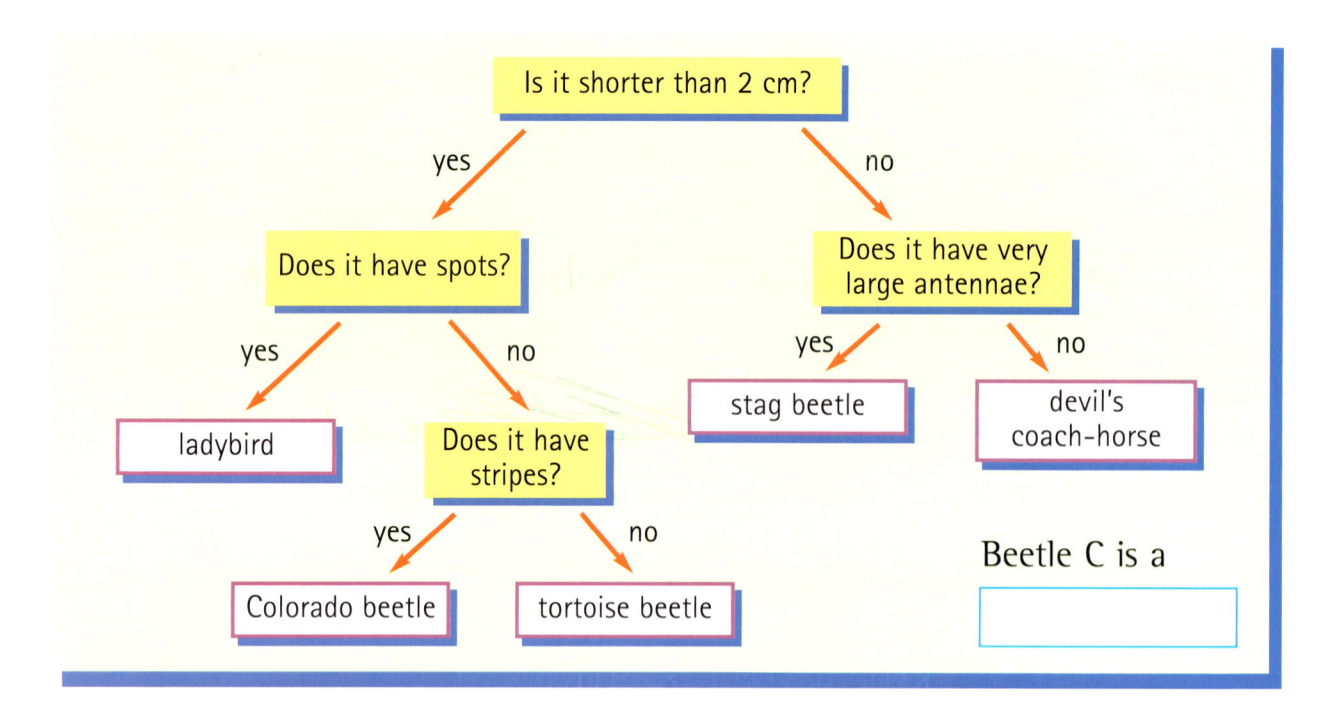

```
                    Is it shorter than 2 cm?
              yes                          no
        Does it have spots?         Does it have very
                                    large antennae?
        yes        no               yes          no
     ladybird   Does it have    stag beetle   devil's
                stripes?                      coach-horse
                yes     no
                                        Beetle C is a
         Colorado beetle  tortoise beetle   ┌─────────┐
                                            └─────────┘
```

(b) Give one difference between a ladybird and a Colorado beetle.

_____

4   Some micro-organisms are useful and some are harmful.

    For each row put a tick in the correct box.

	Useful	Harmful
cold virus		
yeast in bread		
bacteria in plaque		
micro-organisms in compost		

5   Milo has a cold. Nina has told him he must cover his nose and mouth when he sneezes.

    Explain why this is important.

    _____

The human body

Bright sparks!

- Your skeleton protects vital organs, supports your body and allows you to move.
- There are three types of teeth: incisors for cutting and snipping, canines for ripping and tearing and molars for crushing and grinding.
- Your heart pumps blood around your body. Your **pulse** is a measure of your heart rate. It gets quicker and stronger with exercise.

If only Dotty had followed my advice she would not have toothache.

- Always brush your teeth twice a day to get rid of plaque.
- Visit your dentist.
- Don't eat too many sugary foods.

1 (a) The human skeleton protects important parts of the body.

This is a picture of a human skeleton.

Complete the sentences in the boxes. One has been done for you.

The skull protects *the brain*

The ribs protect *the lungs and heart*

The spine protects **the spinal cord.**

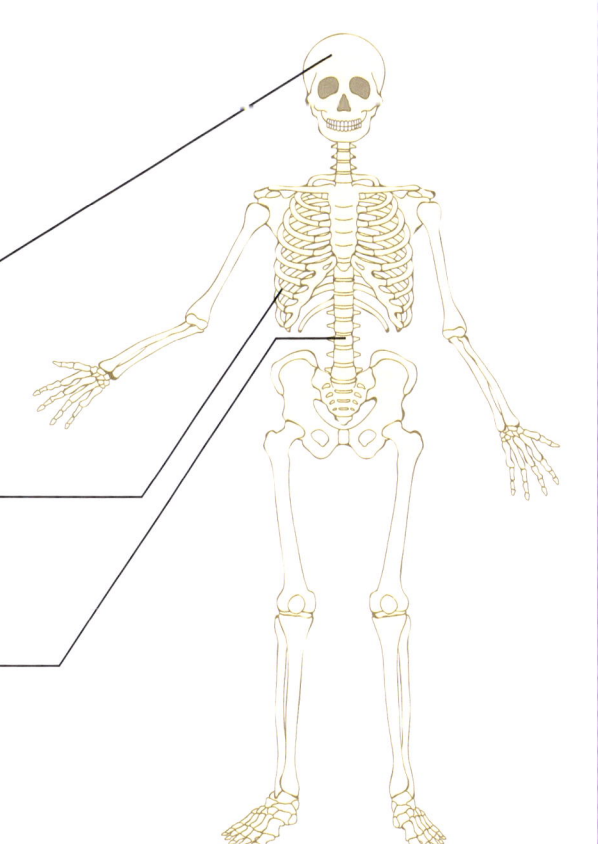

(b) Give ONE other reason why we have a skeleton.

so we donk wer are jelly

(c) This picture shows the different types of adult teeth.

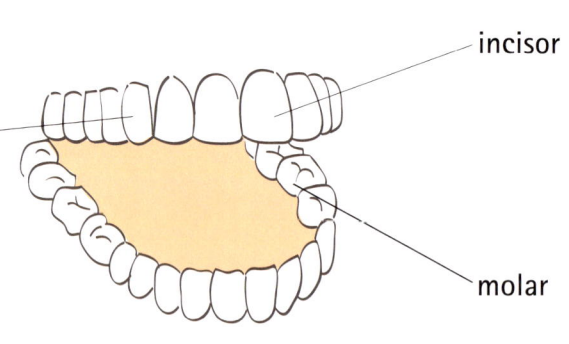

Each type of tooth does a different job.

Complete this table to show the main job for each type of tooth.

Type of tooth	Main job
canine	used for tearing food
incisor	
molar	to chew chewy slugs

2 (a) Two adults were asked about their lifestyle.

A questionnaire was used to collect the results.

Name: Aunt Julie
- Do you smoke? Y ✓ N
- Do you exercise at least three times a week? Y N ✓
- Do you drink alcohol? Y ✓ N
- Do you eat at least five portions of fruit and vegetables a day? Y N ✓

Name: Uncle Tony
- Do you smoke? Y N ✓
- Do you exercise at least three times a week? Y ✓ N
- Do you drink alcohol? Y ✓ N
- Do you eat at least five portions of fruit and vegetables a day? Y ✓ N

Which of them is more likely to develop heart disease?

(b) Give TWO reasons why regular exercise keeps you healthy.

3 (a) Dotty measured her heart rate between 8:00 am and 8:30 am.

She recorded these measurements on a graph.

What was Dotty's heart rate at 8:00 am?

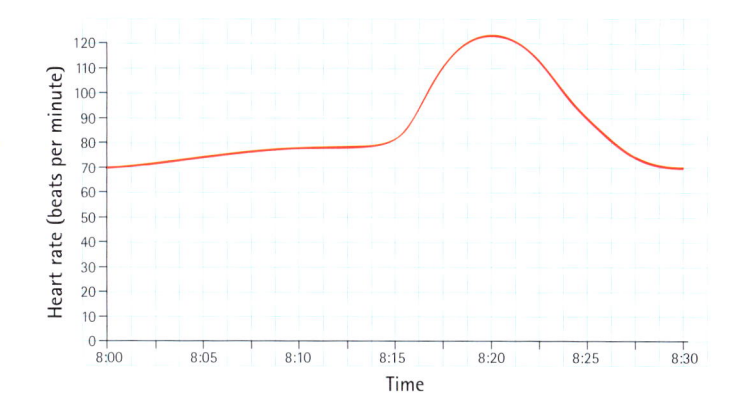

(b) Dotty had to run after a Spydrax who had stolen her new shoes.

Mark a cross on the graph where you think she started running.

(c) What job does the heart do inside the body?

4 (a) The boxes show the weight of a person at different stages of their life.

Draw lines to match each weight with the correct stage of life.

25 kg   60 kg   5 kg   45 kg

baby   teenager   child   adult

(b) Draw bars on the chart to show the weights at each stage of the human life cycle.

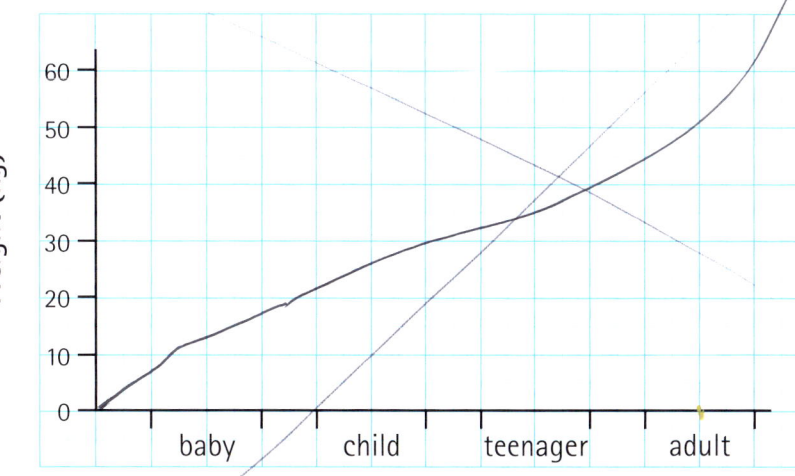

11

Electricity

Bright sparks!

- Only a correctly-wired circuit will let electricity flow. A switch can break this flow by opening or closing a gap in the circuit.
- Some materials, especially metals, let electricity flow through them easily. These are called electrical conductors.

To make a bulb shine brighter in a circuit:
- Add more batteries.
- Shorten the wires.

Simple!

1 (a) Nina has made a circuit.

The circuit contains a battery, a switch, a buzzer and wires.

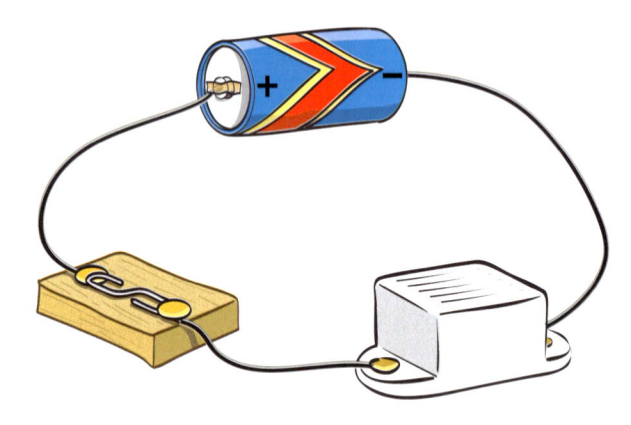

Draw a circuit diagram of Nina's circuit.
Use these symbols.

battery   buzzer   switch

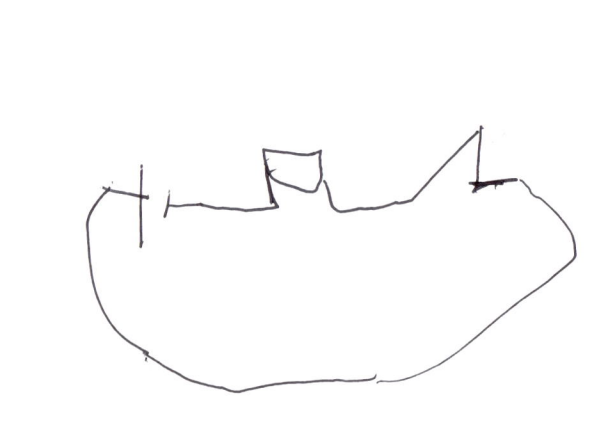

(b) Nina adds another battery to make the buzzer louder.

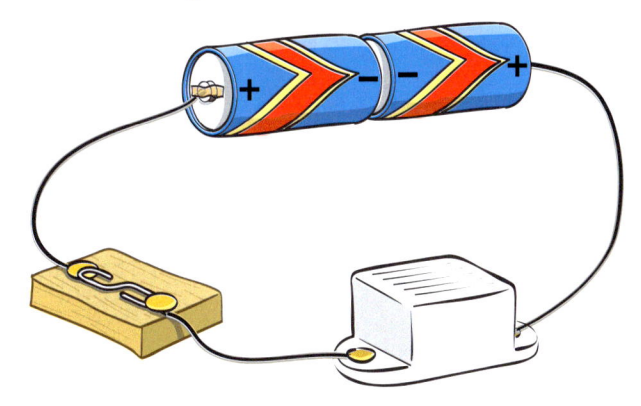

The buzzer does not sound, yet the switch is closed.

What is wrong with Nina's circuit?

_____

(c) Milo makes a circuit using a battery, a bulb, a switch and wires.

Milo wants to make the bulb brighter, but does not have another battery.

Explain how Milo could change his circuit to make the bulb brighter.

_____

2   Dotty wants to test how well different materials conduct electricity.

The picture below shows her circuit.

She connects different materials in the gap one at a time.

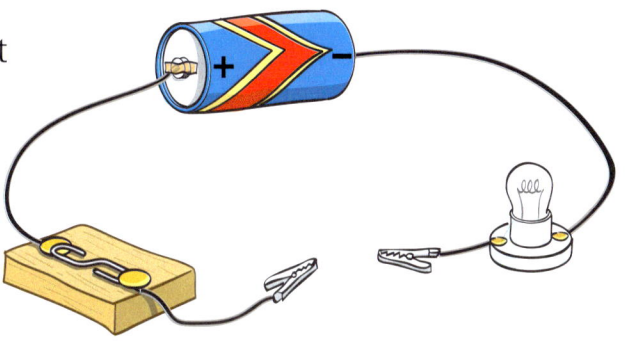

Put a tick next to each material that will conduct electricity.

steel comb	✓	plastic ruler		copper coin	
cardboard tube		matchstick	✓	kitchen foil	✓

13

Forces

Bright sparks!

All forces are either pushes or pulls.

- **Gravity** is the downward pull of the Earth.
- **Friction** is a force which slows or stops one object from moving over another.
- **Upthrust** is the upward push on an object in water.

Zeb says

Magnets can either push or pull.

They have two poles: north and south.

If you put the same poles together they push away or `repel`.

If you put different poles together they pull together or `attract`.

1 (a) Strat has two bar magnets.

The poles are marked N for north and S for south.

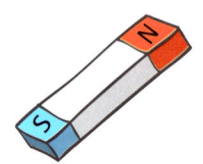

The two magnets are now placed so that they repel each other.

Mark the poles N and S on the diagram below.

(b) Strat puts some small objects on a thin plastic tray. He wants to test which object can be pulled along by a magnet.

Strat places the magnet below an object under the tray and tries to pull it.

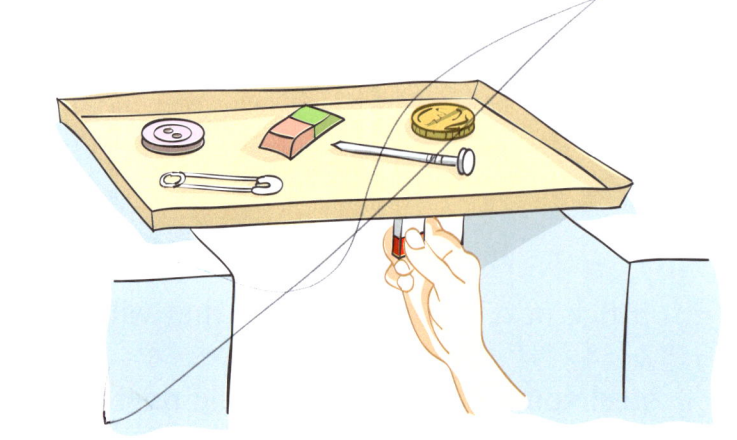

Some of the objects move. Some do not.

Put a tick next to the objects that can be pulled by the magnet.

copper coin ☐ nail ☐ plastic button ☐

eraser ☐ safety pin ☐

(c) Strat has four different magnets and a box of paper clips.

He tests the strength of one of the magnets by seeing how many paper clips it can pick up.

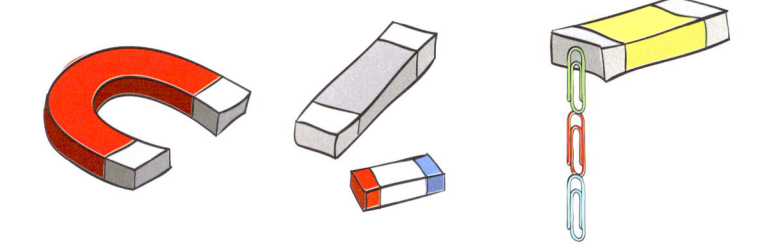

Describe what Strat could do to work out which is the strongest magnet.

2(a) Nina uses a **forcemeter** to weigh a large pebble and a rubber ball.

Write down the weight of the rubber ball.

Large pebble   3 Newtons

Rubber ball   Newtons

(b) Nina now weighs the pebble in water.

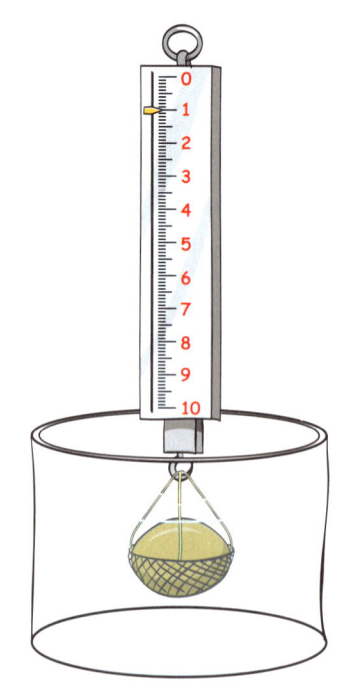

The reading on the forcemeter is now only 1 Newton.

Explain why the pebble weighs less in water than it does in the air.

_____

_____

(c) Nina now weighs the rubber ball in water.

She notices that the ball floats and that the reading on the forcemeter is 0 Newtons.

On the diagram draw **TWO** arrows to show the two forces which are acting on the ball.

3 (a) Dotty has two sheets of paper which are the same size.

She crumples up one sheet to make a ball.

She wants to investigate what will happen when she drops both objects from a height.

Why do you think it is important that Dotty drops both objects at the same time from the same height?

_____

_____

(b) She repeats the experiment more than once. Explain why she does this.

_____

(c) Dotty observes that each time the sheet of paper takes longer to land than the ball.

Give a reason why this happens.

_____

_____

4 Strat and Nina are walking across Sparkley Square which is covered in ice.

Strat is wearing shoes with smooth plastic soles.

Nina is wearing trainers.

Explain why Nina is finding it easier to walk on the ice than Strat.

_____

_____

Light

Bright sparks!

- A **shadow** is formed when an object blocks out the light.
- Moving a light source towards an object makes the shadow smaller.

Light sources

Reflecting light

Zeb says

You need to know the difference between these words:

Opaque – doesn't let any light through

Translucent – lets some light through

Transparent – lets all light through.

1. The picture shows a room in the Malvo's Den.

   Strat has counted **four** light sources in the room.

   Put a circle around each light source.

2 (a) Strat has also found another light source – a torch.

   He shines the torch at his hand and it casts a shadow on the wall behind.

   Explain how the shadow is formed.

18

(b) Strat moves his hand closer to the torch.

What happens to the shadow?

Tick **ONE** box.   gets smaller ☐   gets larger ☐

　　　　　　　　　stays the same ☐   disappears ☐

(c) Strat now uses his torch to test which materials allow light to pass through them.

Complete the table below to predict his results.

Tick **ONE** box in each row.

Material	No light passes through	Allows some light through
Cling film		
Paper hanky		
Kitchen foil		
Thick cardboard		
Tissue paper		

3   Choose the correct word to complete the sentence.

　　　translucent　　　　transparent　　　　opaque

A material that does not let any light pass through it is _____.

4   Strat now uses his torch to investigate materials which reflect light.

He shines his torch on the objects below.

For each picture, put a tick in the box if it reflects the light from Strat's torch.

mirror ☐　　　paper plate ☐　　　CD ☐　　　cushion ☐

Sound and vibration

Bright sparks!

- Sound is caused when particles in a solid, a liquid or a gas vibrate.
- **Pitch** is how high or low a sound is.
- The more energy used to make a sound the louder it will be.

Zeb says

Did you know that sounds can be heard when vibrations from an object reach your ears?

Sound travels very well through the air but not as well through other materials.

1 (a) Dotty and Milo are playing with a set of three tubular bells.

Dotty strikes bell C with a hammer and it makes a sound.

Explain why the bell makes a sound.

_____

_____

(b) How could Dotty make the sound louder?

_____

(c) Dotty hits each bell.

Which bell will make the highest note?

Tick **ONE** box.

A ☐   B ☐   C ☐

What is the relationship between the length of the bell and the pitch of the note?

_____

_____

(d) Milo goes into the room next door.

He can still hear the tubular bells, but they sound quieter.

Explain why the bells sound quieter in the next room.

_____

_____

The Earth and beyond

Bright sparks!

- The Sun, Moon and Earth are all spheres.
- As the Earth **orbits** the Sun it rotates on its tilted axis, causing day and night.
- A shadow is formed when an object blocks the Sun's rays.

What does the word orbit mean?

It's the proper word for travels round.

Zeb says

The Earth orbits the Sun in 365 days – that's a year.

The Moon orbits the Earth in 28 days – about a month.

---

1 (a) The diagram shows the positions of the Earth, Moon and Sun.

Complete the labels to identify the Earth, the Moon and the Sun.

(b) On the diagram draw the orbit of the Earth around the Sun.

(c) How long does it take for the Moon to orbit the Earth?

Tick **ONE** box.

    7 days ☐   28 days ☐   30 days ☐   365 days ☐

(d) What word is used to describe the shape of the Moon?

Tick **ONE** box.

    round ☐   oval ☐   sphere ☐   crescent ☐

2   Look carefully at the diagram of the Sun and the Earth.

In the diagram in which city is it midday (12 o'clock)? _____

3 (a)   Milo is investigating the shadow cast by a lollystick at different times on a sunny day.

He has placed a lollystick on the windowsill and has noted the length and position of the shadow formed.

The diagram shows the shadows at 9 o'clock and 12 o'clock.
The shadow is shortest at 12 o'clock.

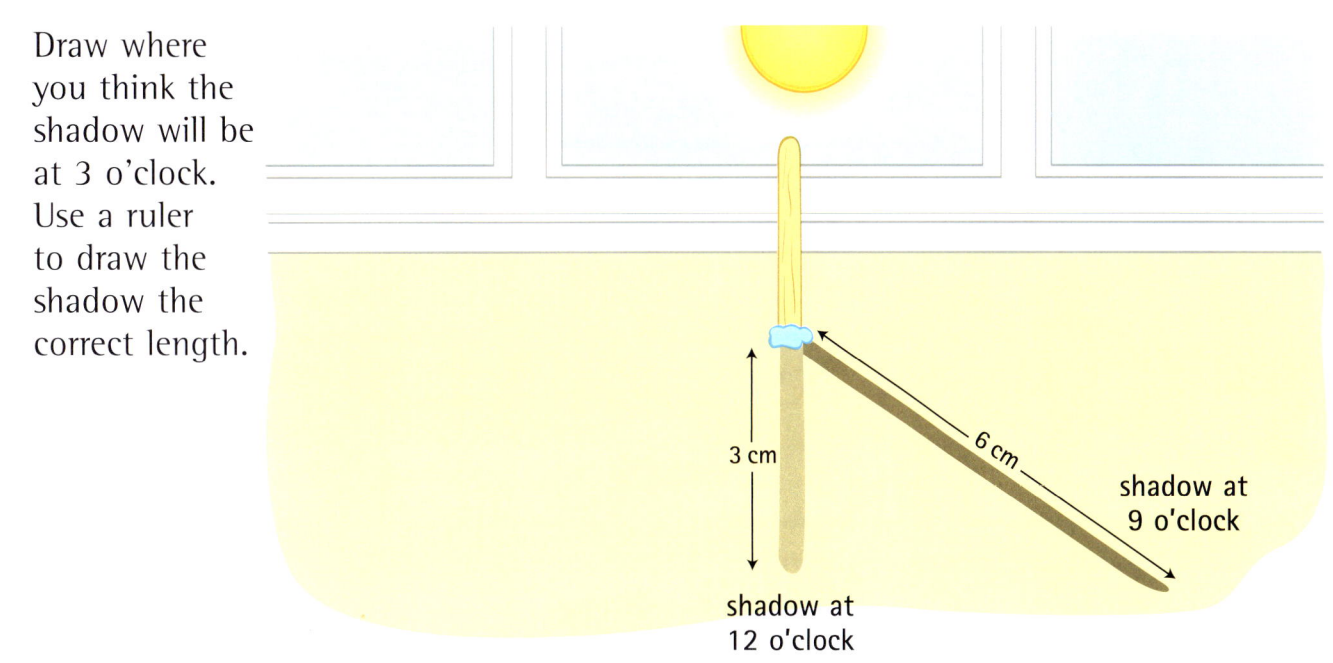

Draw where you think the shadow will be at 3 o'clock. Use a ruler to draw the shadow the correct length.

(b)   Explain why the shadow is shortest at 12 o'clock.

_____

_____

Grouping and classifying materials

Bright sparks!

- All materials are either solid, liquid or gas.
- Materials have properties which make them useful for different jobs.

warm

waterproof

transparent

Zeb says

Did you know that water is the only material on Earth which occurs naturally as a solid (ice), a liquid (water) and a gas (steam)?

1. Strat is investigating the properties of some materials. He is comparing plastic, leather, granite and steel.

   He uses a key to sort the materials.

   Complete the key by writing steel, granite, leather or plastic in the correct boxes in the key.

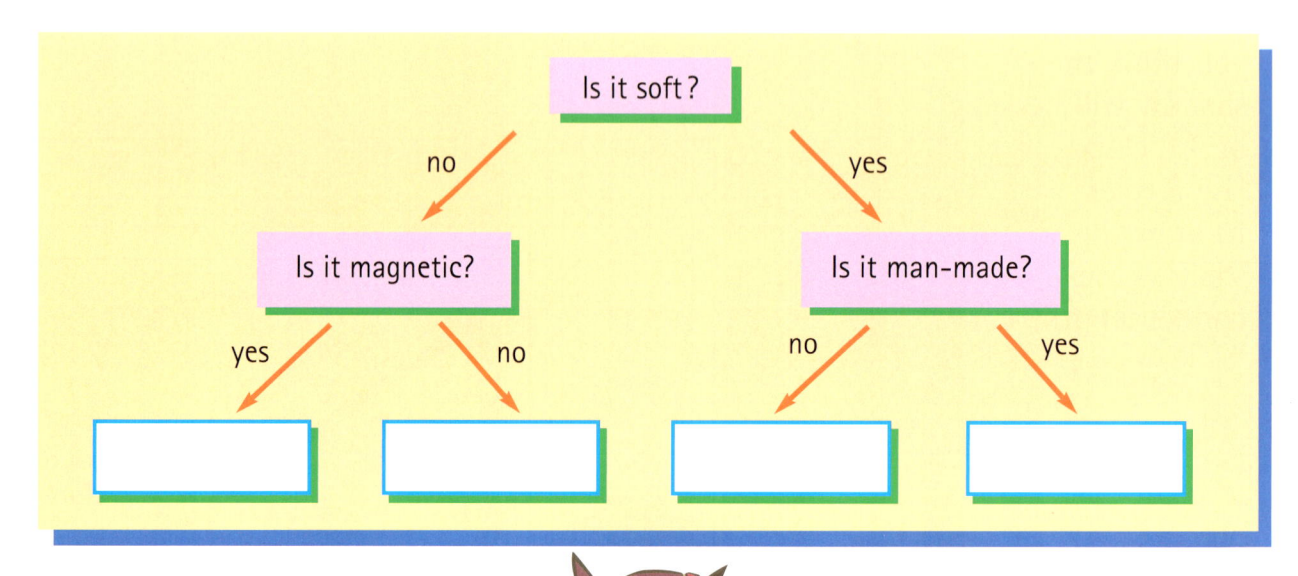

   Is it soft?
   - no → Is it magnetic?
     - yes → ☐
     - no → ☐
   - yes → Is it man-made?
     - no → ☐
     - yes → ☐

2(a) Nina has blown up a paddling pool and filled it with water.

Complete the sentences below using these words: solid, liquid and gas.

The paddling pool is made out of plastic, which is a _____.

Nina has inflated the pool by blowing in air, which is a _____.

The paddling pool is filled with water, which is a _____.

(b) The paddling pool is made from PVC plastic.
Put a tick next to the TWO words which best describe this material.

| waterproof ☐ | permeable ☐ | hard ☐ |
| magnetic ☐ | flexible ☐ | rigid ☐ |

3 Dotty goes into her garden after a heavy rainstorm.

She notices that the heavy clay soil at the back of the garden is very wet and has puddles of water on the surface.

At the other side of the garden, she notices that the sandpit is damp but there are no puddles.

What effect does the size of the sand and clay particles have on their ability to hold water?

_____

4 Write the following materials inside the correct ring.

water   sand
oxygen   oil   milk
carbon dioxide
brick   paper

Solid

Liquid

Gas

25

Changing materials

Bright sparks!

- There are two types of changes to materials.
- A **non-reversible** change is permanent. You can't get your original materials back, e.g. baking a cake, and burning a match.
- A **reversible** change is temporary. You can get your original material back, e.g. melting chocolate then cooling it, and **evaporating** water then **condensing** it.

Zeb says

When it rains the raindrops fall into rivers which flow into the sea. The Sun heats up the seawater and makes it evaporate up into clouds. The clouds move over the hills and the rain falls into the rivers again. This is called the **water cycle**.

1 (a) Nina is making a chocolate chip cake.

Here is a list of the ingredients she needs:

eggs   flour   butter   sugar   chocolate chips

When some foods are warmed on a low heat they just melt.

Which **THREE** of the ingredients will melt if heated on their own?

_____ , _____

and _____

(b) Nina mixes all the ingredients in a food mixer.

She then puts the mixture into a cake tin and places it in a hot oven.

Nina says that baking a cake is non-reversible.

Explain what she means by this.

2 (a) Strat heats some ice cubes in a pan until the ice turns to water.

He then boils the water until he sees steam rising from the pan.

Strat lets the steam cool on the pan lid.

Then he puts the water from the pan into the ice-cube tray and puts it back in the freezer.

The changes to the ice cubes can be shown in a diagram.

Put the **FOUR** words into the correct boxes in the diagram.

evaporates   freezes   condenses   melts

ice

water

water

steam

(b) Tick the word that best describes this type of change.

non-reversible ☐   reversible ☐   boiling ☐

3 Dotty notices that when she breathes on a window, it mists up.

Describe what is happening.

Separating mixtures of materials

Bright sparks!

- You can use a sieve to separate large particles (bits) from a mixture. A filter or filter paper can be used to separate finer particles.
- Substances that dissolve are **soluble** and substances that do not are insoluble.

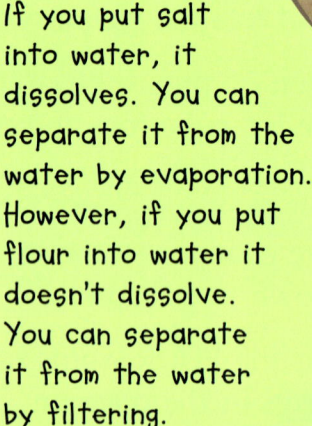

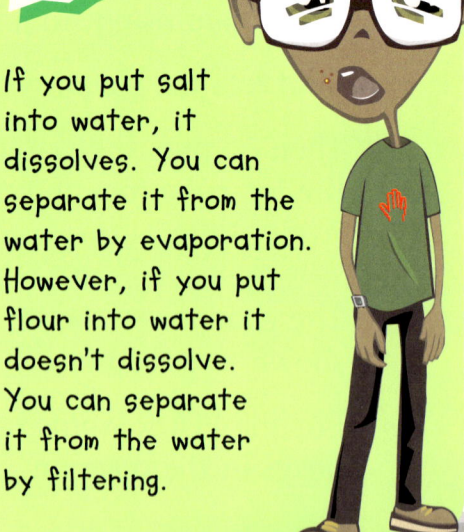

Zeb says

If you put salt into water, it dissolves. You can separate it from the water by evaporation. However, if you put flour into water it doesn't dissolve. You can separate it from the water by filtering.

1 (a) Nina has been experimenting with mixtures. She mixed together some salt and some sand in a jar of water.

Then she challenged Milo to separate the sand and salt from the water.

Nina gave Milo the equipment shown opposite.

Explain how Milo can first separate the sand from the mixture using some of the equipment.

_____

_____

(b) Now explain how Milo can remove the salt from the remaining mixture using some of the equipment.

_____

_____

(c) What is this process called? _____

Science Key Stage 2 Practice test

Instructions

Read this carefully.

Answers

This shows where you will need to put your answer.

For some questions, you may need to draw an answer instead of writing one.

You have **45 minutes** for this test.

1 Habitats

(a) Draw lines joining each creature to its habitat.

garden spider

newt

earthworm

woodlouse

1a

2 marks

(b) Look at the picture of the grey heron.

The heron is a large wading bird.
It lives near or in shallow water.
It feeds on small fish.

1b(i)

1 mark

Describe **TWO** features of the heron which make it suited to its habitat.

1b(ii)

(i) _____

1 mark

(ii) _____

30

2 Keeping healthy

(a) Jonathan notices a sticky white coating on his teeth when he wakes up in the morning.

What is the name of this sticky coating?

Tick ONE box.

sugar ☐   acid ☐   bacteria ☐   plaque ☐

2a — 1 mark

(b) Jonathan is making a poster about looking after your teeth.

Complete the poster with TWO more ways to keep your teeth healthy.

Keep your teeth healthy!

- Brush your teeth twice a day.
-
-

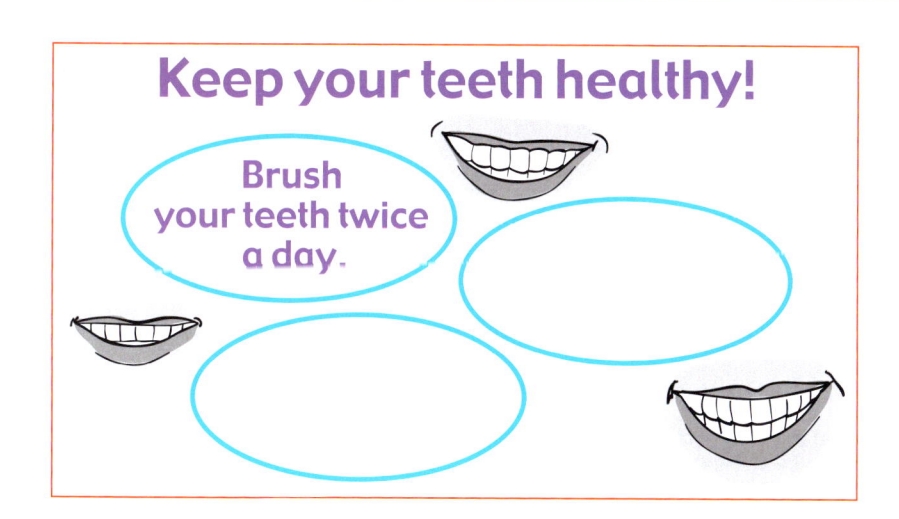

2b — 2 marks

(c) Some lifestyle choices are good for the heart. Some choices are bad.

For each row put a tick in the correct box.

Lifestyle choice	Good for your heart	Bad for your heart
Regular exercise		
Eating fatty foods		
Smoking cigarettes		
Eating a balanced diet		

2c — 2 marks

31

3 Making drinks in the kitchen

(a) Danielle is making some lemonade using lemon juice, sugar lumps and water.

The first step is to dissolve the sugar lumps in the water.

(i) **Suggest TWO factors which will affect how quickly the sugar dissolves.**

1 _____

2 _____

(ii) Danielle then adds the lemon juice to her sugar solution.

She notices that there are some lemon pips in her lemonade.

What piece of equipment could Danielle use to separate the pips from the lemonade?

_____

(b) Adam is making a cup of coffee. He pours boiling water into the cup.

Adam notices that when he holds a spoon over the cup of coffee water droplets are formed on the spoon.

(i) **What word describes this process?**

Tick **ONE** box.

evaporation ☐   condensation ☐   filtering ☐   melting ☐

(ii) Adam leaves the spoon in the cup for five minutes.

When he takes the spoon out it is very hot.

Explain why the spoon is now hot.

_____

4 Thermal insulation

(a) Jack is doing an experiment to find out which materials keep iced water cool the longest.

He has three plastic cups. He puts an equal amount of iced water into each cup. He then wraps each cup in a different material.

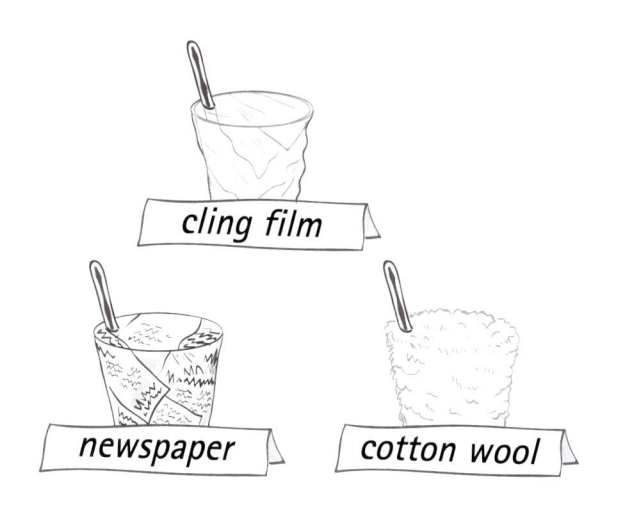

Jack measures the temperature every 20 minutes and records his results.

Material	Temperature (°C) after:					
	0 mins	20 mins	40 mins	60 mins	80 mins	100 mins
cling film	0	2	4	6	8	10
newspaper	0	3	6	9	11	13
cotton wool	0	1	2	4	6	7

Jack thinks he has made his experiment a fair test.

Give ONE way in which he has done this.

_____

_____

(b) Which material is the best thermal insulator? ☐

(c) Use the results of Jack's experiment to explain your answer to (b).

_____

_____

(d) Jack decides to plot his results for the cup covered in cotton wool.

Use the results from the table above to complete the graph.

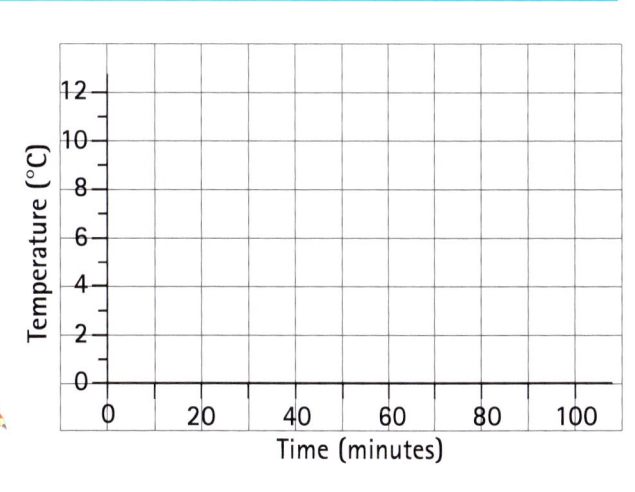

5 Photographs

(a) Randeep wants to develop some photographs in her bedroom.

She needs to block out all sunlight from the room.

She decides to cover the window with a sheet of black tissue paper.

Explain whether Randeep's choice of material is a good one.

_____

_____

(b) Which word best describes the material Randeep used to cover the window?

translucent ☐   transparent ☐   opaque ☐   dense ☐

(c) Randeep has taken four photographs of the bird table in her garden.

She has taken them at different times of the day.

A   B   C   D

| 8 o'clock in the morning | | noon | |

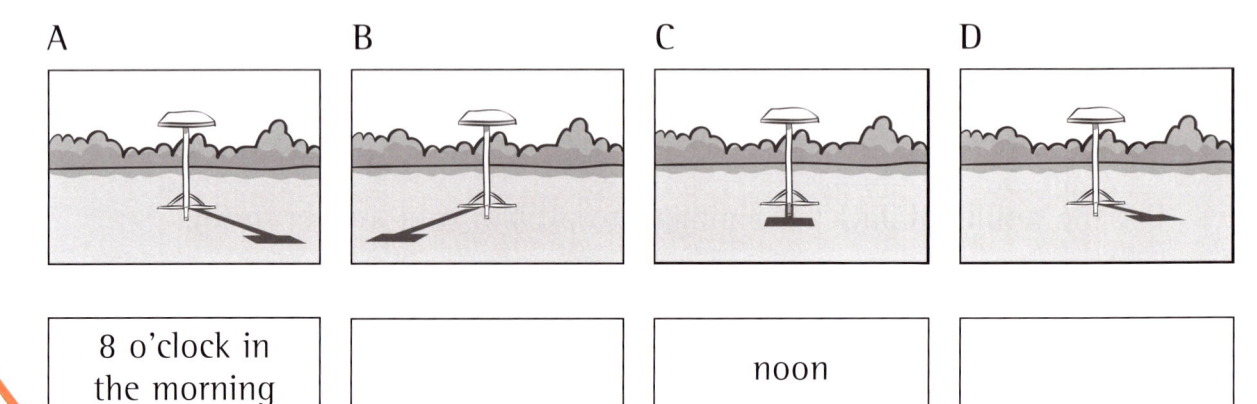

Photograph A was taken at 8 o'clock in the morning.

Photograph C was taken at noon.

Suggest times at which Photograph B and D were taken.

6 Electric circuits

(a) Mark has made three electric circuits. Each circuit has a lamp.

He has drawn a circuit diagram for each one.

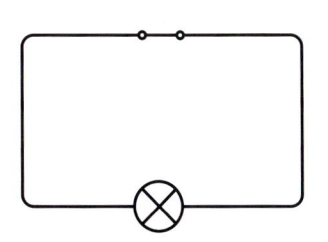

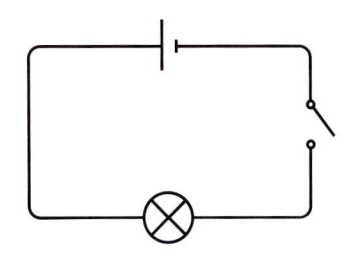

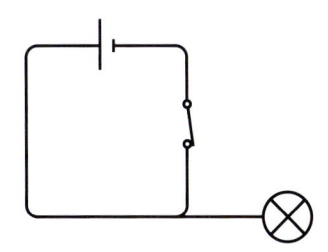

None of the bulbs light up.

Explain what is wrong with each circuit.

1 _____

2 _____

3 _____

6a

3 marks

(b) Mark has this equipment.

He wants to build a circuit which will light up a single bulb as brightly as possible.

It must also be possible to switch the bulb on and off.

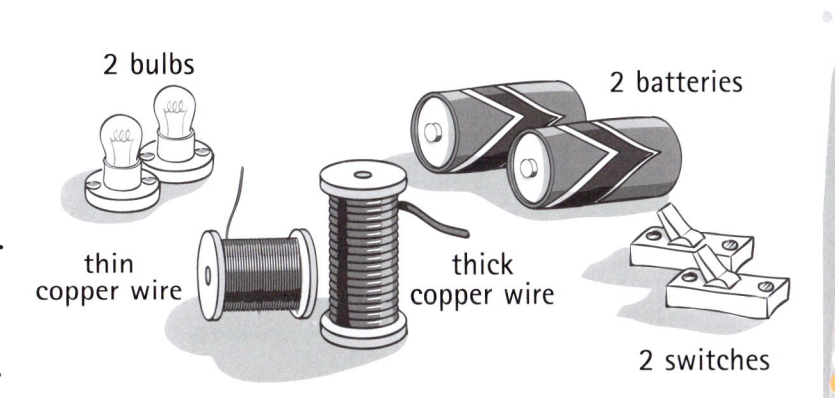

2 bulbs
thin copper wire
thick copper wire
2 batteries
2 switches

Describe how you would build a suitable circuit.

_____

_____

6b

2 marks

7 Forces

(a) Hannah has measured some objects using a forcemeter.

She writes her results in a table.

Object	Weight in Newtons (N)
cup	4
candle	2
brick	8
tin	3

(i) Which object produced the most force?

Tick ONE box.

cup ☐   candle ☐   brick ☐   tin ☐

(ii) Tick ONE box to complete the sentence.

As the weight added on the end of the forcemeter gets heavier, the spring

becomes longer ☐   stays the same length ☐

becomes shorter ☐   snaps ☐

(b) Hannah now weighs the brick in water and in salt water.

She writes her results in a table.

Object	Weight of brick in air (N)	Weight of brick in water (N)	Weight of brick in salt water (N)
Brick	8	5	3

(i) Name the TWO forces acting on the brick when it is weighed in water.

_____ and _____

(ii) Explain why the brick weighs less in salt water than in normal water.

_____

_____

8 Flowering plants

(a) Draw lines to match the correct statement to each part of the flower.

One has been done for you.

Statements	Parts
Make food for the flower.	roots
Male part of the flower. It produces pollen.	petal
Female part of the flower.	stamen
Takes up water and nutrients. Anchors the plant.	leaves
Attracts insects to the plant.	stigma

(The "Attracts insects to the plant" box is matched to "petal".)

(b) After pollination, seeds from a plant can be dispersed (scattered) in different ways.

Describe **TWO** ways that seeds can be dispersed.

(i) _____

(ii) _____

9 Changes

(a) Fazrul is melting chocolate.

He records the mass of the chocolate over 10 minutes.

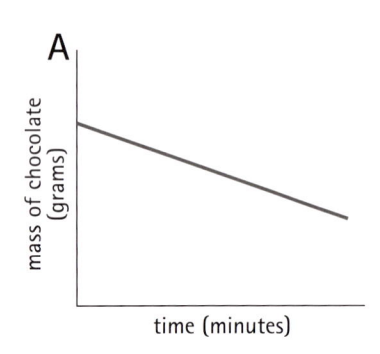

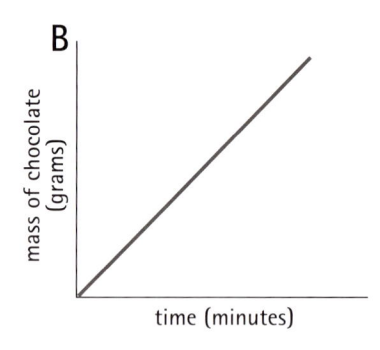

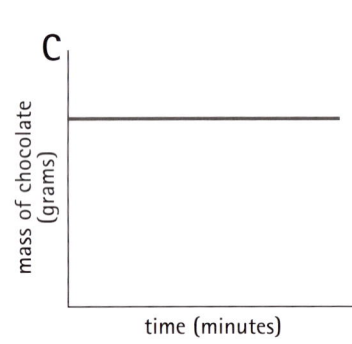

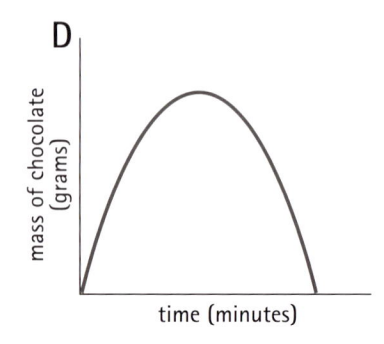

A — mass of chocolate (grams) vs time (minutes): line decreasing

B — mass of chocolate (grams) vs time (minutes): line increasing

C — mass of chocolate (grams) vs time (minutes): horizontal line

D — mass of chocolate (grams) vs time (minutes): curve up then down

Which graph best shows the results? Graph ☐

(b) Lauren lights a tealight candle.

She notices that some of the wax melts to form a liquid.

Lauren records the mass of the tealight over 10 minutes.

She lets the tealight burn for one hour before she blows it out.

Then she notices that half of the wax is missing.

(i) Explain what has happened to the missing wax.

_____

_____

(ii) Which word best describes the change that has taken place?

☐

Sample test questions and answers

Here are three questions selected from past National Tests. These questions were chosen to given an insight into the way questions are actually marked and the errors that children tend to make.

KS2 2002, Test A

3(a) Jack gets out of the bath. He dries himself with a towel.

> Why is towelling a good material to dry himself with?

In this question your child needs to understand that it is the way the material of the towel soaks up water - its absorbency - which is the important factor.

The mark would be awarded for answers such as:
- the towel is absorbent
- it soaks up water
- it absorbs water
- it takes in water.

However, a mark would not be awarded for the following answers:
- it is soft – true, but this answer does not relate to the water
- the towel is flexible – true, but it is not the property mentioned in the question
- it is like a sponge – this compares with another material rather than mentioning the property itself
- it sucks up water – the right idea, but not a proper scientific word in this case.

KS2 2002, Test A

6(c) Meena reads in a book that the human heart beats about 4300 times an hour at resting rate.

Meena says: 'I want to check this information, but I cannot measure my heart beat for an hour.'

> How can Meena find out **quickly** if her heart beats about 4300 times an hour?

This question, whilst on the topic of the heart, is actually testing your child's approach to scientific enquiry. The question is about finding a practical solution to a problem.

The mark would be awarded for answers such as:
- measure it (pulse) for a minute and then times by 60
- she could take her pulse for a little while and times it to get the number for one hour
- she could measure her heart beat for 6 minutes and multiply by 10.

A suitable answer must include reference to the pulse, measuring for a short time (less than 6 minutes) and multiplying to get the pulse for an hour. Actual values or calculations do not have to be present.

However, the mark would not be awarded for answers such as:
- she measures her heart beat/pulse – no reference to times
- she measures her pulse for one minute – no reference to how this would then be used to get the number per hour.

KS2 2002, Test B

3(c) Mohab makes a poster. Complete the poster.

Write **two** other ways that people can look after their teeth.

LOOK AFTER YOUR TEETH

1 Brush your teeth with toothpaste twice a day.

2 _____

3 _____

This question is testing your child's knowledge of caring for teeth and is worth two marks. A mark would awarded for each different way suggested.

Suitable answers would be:
- not eating sugary foods
- don't eat acidic foods
- use a toothpick
- chew sugar-free gum
- use a fluoride toothpaste
- brush your teeth thoroughly
- don't smoke
- drink water containing fluoride.
- do not drink fizzy drinks
- visit the dentist (regularly)
- use dental floss
- change your toothbrush regularly
- wear a gum shield during some sports
- brush your teeth before bed or after meals
- eat foods or drinks with calcium

Answers which simply repeat information given in the question such as 'brush teeth' or 'use toothpaste' would not be awarded a mark. Other unsuitable answers such as 'suck your thumb' don't get a mark.

KS2 2002, Test B

4(c) The children make ice lollies of different sizes.
They time how long the lollies take to melt.
Here are their results.

Volume of lolly (cm³)	Time taken to melt (minutes)
30	200
40	230
50	255
60	275
70	295

Describe the link between the volume of the lolly and the time it takes to melt.

This question is worth two marks so your child would have to provide a detailed answer. Two marks would be awarded if your child has understood the general relationship between volume and time, that is, the greater the volume of the lolly, the longer it takes to melt.

Suitable answers could be:
- the more ice in the lolly, the longer it takes to melt
- the less ice in the lolly, the shorter time it takes to melt
- the longer or bigger the lolly, the longer it takes to melt.

One mark would be awarded for answers which make **two specific** comparisons, for example 'small ice lollies melt quickly and big ice lollies melt slowly'. One mark would also be awarded for a **single** comparison such as 'little ice lollies melt the quickest'.

However, no marks would be awarded for answers which change one of the quantities (volume and time); e.g. 'the bigger the lolly, the colder it is' (referring to temperature rather than time); 'the smaller the lolly, the easier it will melt' (not concerned with 'ease' of melting).

KS2 2002, Test B

6(b) Carina makes a drum by stretching a balloon over the top of a jam jar. She hits the stretched balloon with a beater. It makes a sound.

She pulls the balloon more tightly over the jar.
This changes the pitch of the sound.

> Describe what pitch means.
> How does the pitch change when the balloon is tighter?

The first part of the question is testing whether your child knows that pitch describes how high or low a note is.

A mark would be awarded for answers such as:
- how high the note is
- how low the sound is
- high and low.

The mark would also be awarded for answers which correctly mention frequency (a knowledge of which is not required at KS2), e.g. 'frequency', 'different frequencies'.

The mark would not be awarded for answers which contain incorrect science such as 'how loud the sound is', 'the volume', or incomplete answers such as 'low', 'high' or 'tone of the sound'.

The second part of the question tests your child's understanding of how the pitch changes.

A mark would be awarded for answers such as:
- the pitch rises
- makes a higher note
- the pitch goes up
- frequency increases
- faster vibrations (beyond KS2 requirements).

A mark would not be awarded for the answer 'the pitch is high', as it does not mention how the pitch has changed.

Answers to practice questions

Green plants

1 **(a)** Stamen. **(b)** The missing labels are, in this order: petal; stem; leaf. **(c)** Answers should refer clearly to the roots either anchoring, keeping in place or fixing the plant in the soil; or soaking up or transporting water and/or minerals to the plant.

2 **(a)** Answers should mention that the seeds are light; the seeds have feathers/are feathery; or the seeds look like parachutes. An answer such as 'the seeds are easily blown by the wind' is not acceptable as it is simply rephrasing the question. **(b)** Producer. All plants are producers because they make their own food.

3 **(a)** C. **(b)** The reason is that plants need sufficient, but not too much, water and light to grow well.

Living things and their environments

1 **(a)** D. **(b)** Reason: slugs prefer damp conditions to prevent drying out and to give cover from predators. **(c)** Cabbage, slug, thrush, kestrel. (All must be in the correct order.) **(d)** Cabbage.

2 Grow, reproduce and feed.

3 **(a)** Tortoise beetle. (Make sure your child is confident using keys to deduce such answers.) **(b)** The ladybird has spots, the Colorado beetle has stripes (not spots). Or: The ladybird has very small antennae, the Colorado beetle has larger antennae. Answers must refer to both beetles.

4 Useful: yeast in bread; micro-organisms in compost. Harmful: cold virus; bacteria in plaque.

5 Answers should reflect that Milo needs to cover his nose and mouth when sneezing because the germs/virus/cold can travel/spread through the air and be picked up/breathed in by other people.

The human body

1 **(a)** The skull protects the brain. The ribs protect the heart and/or lungs. Your child may give other organs such as eyes for the skull. **(b)** Answers should reflect that the skeleton lets/allows/helps us to move; keeps us standing upright; supports the body. (Do not allow any answers which refer to protecting organs, since this was given in the first part of the question.)

(c) Incisor: used for chopping, cutting, slicing or nibbling food. Molar: used for grinding, chewing, crunching, smashing or mashing food. (Do not allow bite, as this is the job of all teeth.)

2 **(a)** Aunt Julie. **(b)** Answers should state: makes the lungs, heart, bones or muscles strong or work better (each counts as one); uses up food stores, or burns calories; helps you sleep well; improves coordination. (Marks will not be awarded for repeating words used in the question, e.g. makes the heart healthy.)

3 **(a)** 70 beats per minute, or simply the number 70. **(b)** To answer this question your child should be aware that heart rate increases with exercise. The part of the line between 8:15 and 8:20 shows a rapid increase in heart rate to indicate an increase in activity. The cross should be on the line somewhere between 8:15 and 8:20. (Accept the cross on the time axis, but not on the heart rate axis.) **(c)** Answers should reflect that the heart pumps blood around the body; accept the heart **sends**, **pushes** or **forces** blood around the body. The key words here are **pumps** and **blood**. The use of any other verb rather than **pumps** must be accompanied by a phrase such as: **around the body**.

4 **(a)** 5 kg baby
25 kg child
45 kg teenager
60 kg adult
(b) Your child's bar chart should look like this:

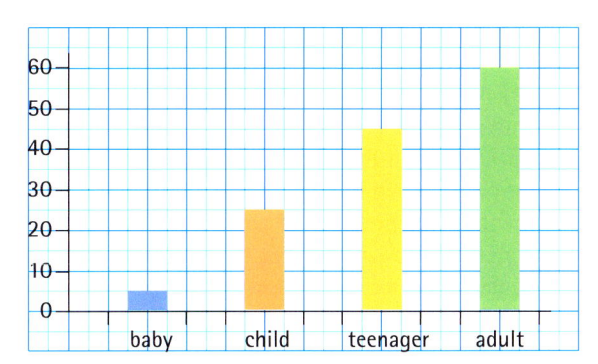

The bars must be within 2 mm of the correct height. Encourage your child to use a ruler and pencil.

Electricity

1 **(a)** Your child's circuit should look like this:

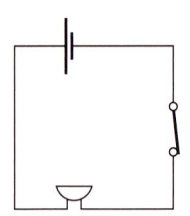

The wires may be drawn as straight or curved lines but it is essential that these lines touch the components and that there are no gaps. The switch must be in the closed position.

(b) One of the batteries is connected the wrong way round; terminals must be connected with positive to negative. **(c)** Shortening the wires. (Answers which involve other components or wires are not allowed.)

2 Steel comb, copper coin, kitchen foil.

Forces

1 **(a)** The diagram should show either:
N S S N   or   S N N S.
(b) The magnet will pull the iron nail and the steel safety pin (only iron and steel are magnetic). (Both need to be correct.) **(c)** Strat could record how many paper clips each magnet picks up. The magnet that picks up the longest string of paper clips is the strongest. Your child must mention that the strongest magnet will pick up the most paper clips.

2 **(a)** 1.6 Newtons. **(b)** The pebble weighs less in water than in air because the upwards force or upthrust from the water cancels out part of the weight or force due to gravity. Your child must mention the presence of an upwards force from the water and how it reduces, takes away or cancels some of the weight or downwards force.
(c) Arrows should be drawn as shown in the diagram below. The arrows must be vertical but do not need to be in line with each other. They must be roughly the same size.

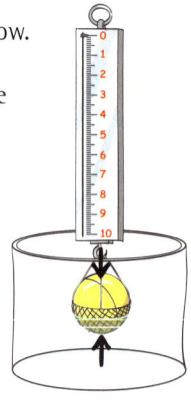

3 **(a)** Answers should refer to ensuring that a fair test takes place, e.g. If the objects are dropped from different heights it will be difficult to compare how quickly each lands. **(b)** To make sure that her results are the same each time. **(c)** This is because there is greater air resistance acting on the sheet of paper, as it has a bigger surface area than the ball; hence it falls more slowly. The ball is more streamlined, so the force from air resistance is small; hence it falls more quickly. Your child should appreciate that, although the two objects weigh the same, and the force due to gravity is therefore the same, the force due to air resistance is greater for the sheet of paper because of its larger surface area.

4 Answers could be that 'Nina's trainers have a better grip than Strat's', or 'Nina's trainers have more friction than Strat's smooth soles', or 'two smooth surfaces rubbing together do not give as much friction as a rough surface on a smooth one'. (Do not allow answers such as 'smooth soles slide more easily than rough soles' as this is simply rephrasing the question.)

Light

1 Computer, lamp, candle, sunlight. Your child may circle the mirror or glass table. These are not light sources, as they simply reflect light.

2 **(a)** Correct answers must refer to blocking the light and the absence of light causing a dark area, e.g. 'Strat's hand blocks the light so there is a dark shape behind it' or 'The light cannot pass through Strat's hand, so a shadow is cast where the light can't reach.' **(b)** Gets larger. **(c)** No light passes through: kitchen foil; thick cardboard.
Allows some light through: cling film; paper hanky; tissue paper.

3 Opaque.

4 The mirror and CD.

Sound and vibration

1 **(a)** The bell vibrates, causing the air inside and around it to vibrate. These vibrations are picked up by our ears. This is how the bell makes the sound. Your child's answer should mention vibration or sound waves travelling. 'It vibrates' is not enough, as some reference to the bell, air and ear must be made.
(b) Hitting the bell harder or with more force.

(c) C. A smaller or shorter vibrating object makes a higher note; a short bell vibrates faster, making a higher note.
(d) The answer should reflect that the bells sound quieter because the wall absorbs some of the sound; sound does not travel very well through bricks, wall or plaster; sound does not travel through a wall as well as through air.

The Earth and beyond

1 (a) Your child's diagram should be labelled as shown below:

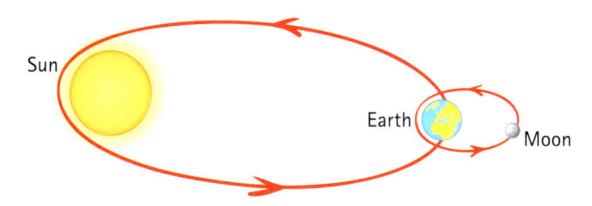

(All three labels must be in the correct places.)
(b) The orbit should be elliptical but does not have to be perfect. The curve should 'cut through' the Earth. Arrows should be anticlockwise, but do not penalise if clockwise or omitted. (c) 28 days.
(d) Sphere.

2 New York.

3 (a) The shadow at 3 o'clock should be about the same length as, and on the opposite side and at a similar angle to, the shadow at 9 o'clock, as shown in the diagram. The shadow is shortest as the Sun is directly overhead and at its highest in the sky.

(b) Shadows are shortest in the middle of the day when the Sun is at its highest, and longest at sunrise and sunset, as the Sun is lower in the sky.

Grouping and classifying materials

1 (a) Reading along from left to right: steel, granite, leather and plastic.

2 (a) Plastic is a solid, air is a gas and water is a liquid. (b) Plastic is waterproof and flexible.

3 Possible answers: sand has finer particles than clay soil, so it lets the water through more easily; sand has more air gaps than clay soil, so it soaks through more easily; water drains through sand more quickly than clay soil.

4 Solid: sand; brick; paper. Liquid: water; oil; milk. Gas: oxygen; carbon dioxide.

Changing materials

1 (a) Butter, sugar and chocolate chips.
(b) It is a permanent change; you cannot get the ingredients back out of the cake.

2 (a) ice – melts
water – evaporates
steam – condenses
water – freezes
(b) Reversible.

3 Your child must use the word **condense** in this answer, e.g. 'The water in Dotty's warm breath **condenses** on the cold window'.

Separating mixtures of materials

1 (a) Milo should pour the mixture through the filter paper and funnel. The sand will be left in the paper and the liquid collected in the pan. Your child must mention the use of the **filter paper** and **funnel**.
(b) Milo should put the liquid in the pan on the cooking ring and heat it until the water evaporates. The salt will be left in the pan. The answer must refer to using the cooking ring as a source of heat. It is not essential to mention the term evaporate here, but your child should explain that the water will turn to steam or boil away but not disappear.
(c) Evaporation.

Answers to practice test

Habitats

1 **(a)** Links should be garden spider - bushes; newt - pond; earthworm - soil; woodlouse - wood. (Deduct a mark for each incorrect answer.)
(b) Answers could include: it has a long bill or beak for catching fish; it has a long neck so that it can reach down into the water to catch food; it has long legs so that it can stand in shallow water; it has waterproof feathers so that it can live in water. (Award one mark for each correct answer. Each answer must state a feature **and** what it is used for. Do not allow general features such as: it has wings, a beak or legs.)

Keeping healthy

2 **(a)** The sticky coating is plaque. (If your child has ticked the box for plaque but has also ticked another, do not award the mark; only one tick is allowed. If your child has ticked an incorrect box and attempted to erase it or cross it out, this must be clearly shown.) **(b)** Suggestions could include: floss your teeth; use a toothpick; visit your dentist regularly (or twice a year or every few months); don't eat too many sweets, sugar, sugary foods or fizzy drinks; drink water with fluoride; use a toothpaste with fluoride; chew sugar-free gum; use a gum shield for sports.
(Award one mark each for two different statements. Do not allow vague statements such as 'eat good food' or any form of repetition of either the statement given in the question or one of your child's own suggestions.)
(c) Good for your heart: regular exercise; eating a balanced diet.
Bad for your heart: eating fatty foods; smoking cigarettes.
(Deduct a mark for each incorrect box ticked.)

Making drinks in the kitchen

3 **(a) (i)** The size of the lumps and the temperature of the water are the two main factors. (Award one mark for stirring/keeping still.)
(ii) A sieve, strainer or filter would separate the pips from the lemonade.
(b) (i) This process is **condensation**.
(ii) Answers must refer to **heat transfer** or **conduction**: metal is a good thermal conductor of heat; the metal transfers heat through the spoon; the coffee heats up the spoon and travels to the handle; the heat travels up the handle. (Do not allow answers such as 'because the coffee is hot'.)

Thermal insulation

4 **(a)** Jack's experiment is fair because: the cups are all the same size; equal amounts of iced water are used; the temperature has been taken at the same time for each cup; the temperature has been taken at regular intervals.
(b) Cotton wool is the best insulator.
(c) Answers should refer to the fact that the temperature for cotton wool at every reading is less than/colder than the other two. This suggests that the cotton wool is keeping heat out of the cup better than the other two materials.
(d) Your child's graph should look like this:

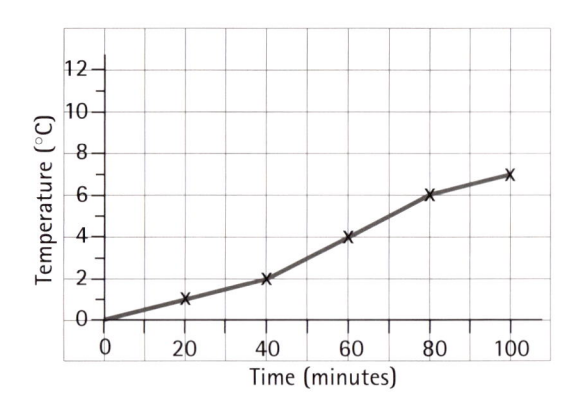

(Award one mark for at least three correctly plotted points and two marks if all are correctly plotted.)

46

Photographs

5 (a) The answer must state that it is not suitable because the tissue paper will let some light through.
(b) A material which only lets some light through is **translucent**.
(c) B – a time between 4 and 6 pm.
D – a time between 10 and 11 am.

(Deduct one mark for each incorrect answer.)

Electric circuits

6 (a) circuit 1: no battery
circuit 2: switch is not closed
circuit 3: the bulb is not within the closed circuit.
(b) Answers should describe a circuit with two batteries, (short) thin wires, one bulb and one switch. (Award one mark for any two of these features and two marks for all four.)

Forces

7 (a)(i) The brick produces the most force.
(ii) The spring becomes longer.
(b)(i) The forces are **gravity** and **upthrust**.
(ii) The answer should indicate that there is more upthrust from the salt water so the salt water pushes the brick up more. Do not accept answers such as 'because the water has salt dissolved in it', 'because the chart tells you this', or 'the salt water is denser'; although the latter is correct, this answer does not explain the effect this has on the weight.

Flowering plants

8 (a) Make food for the flower – leaves
Male part of the flower – stamen
Female part of the flower – stigma
Takes up water and nutrients – roots
(Deduct one mark for each incorrect answer.)
(b) Possible answers include: by animals; animals carrying seeds on their fur or feet; seeds in animal droppings; by wind blowing light seeds; by explosion of pods or seeds; by water; floating down rivers. (Award one mark for each method.)

Changes

9 (a) Graph C best shows the results.
The chocolate is melting which is simply a change in its physical state. Its mass stays the same so the graph showing a constant mass over time (horizontal line) is the correct one.
(b)(i) The wax has evaporated into the air as the candle burned. Your child's answer should refer to **burning** or **evaporating**. Do not allow an answer which refers to the wax disappearing or melting.
(ii) non-reversible

Awarding a level for the practice test

There are 40 possible marks on the test. Compare your child's score with the figures in the table below and read off the corresponding level. The marks required for each level are based on those used to determine levels in the KS2 National Tests. Most pupils are expected to achieve Level 4 in the National Tests.

Level	Score
N	8 or less
2	9-10
3	11-19
4	20-31
5	32-40

Glossary

adaption	the way in which a living thing is suited to its conditions	permeable	describes something that lets water through
air resistance	a force that slows things down as they travel through the air	photosynthesis	the way that green plants make their food using sunlight
attract	to draw towards	pitch	how high or low a sound is
carnivore	a meat eater	pollination	the process by which pollen gets to the female part of a plant
carpel	the female part of the flower		
condense	to turn from gas into liquid		
consumer	a living thing, usually an animal, that gets its food from others	predator	an animal that eats other animals
		prey	an animal eaten by another
disperse	to scatter (seeds)	producer	a living thing that produces its own food
evaporate	to turn from liquid to gas		
forcemeter	an instrument used to measure forces	pulse	a measure of how quickly a heart beats
friction	a force that tries to stop things sliding against each other; it also produces heat	repel	to drive away
		reproduction	the process by which living things have offspring
germinate	to start to grow from a seed into a plant	reversible	a change which can be altered
gravity	a downward pull of the Earth towards its centre	shadow	formed when an object blocks out light
habitat	the home of a plant or animal	soluble	a substance which can be dissolved
herbivore	a plant eater		
impermeable	something that does not allow water through	solution	a solid dissolved in a liquid
		stamen	the male part of the flower
invertebrate	an animal without a backbone	translucent	describes something that lets some light through
microbe	a microscopic living thing		
non-reversible	a change which cannot be altered	transparent	describes something that lets all light through
nutrients	the chemicals in food needed for growth	upthrust	an upward push on an object in water
omnivore	a plant and meat eater	vertebrate	an animal with a backbone
opaque	describes something that does not let any light through	water cycle	the way water evaporates from the sea into the atmosphere, condenses and returns to the Earth as rain or snow
orbit	the path of one object around another in space		